BUSINESS
FRANCE

D0727763

BUSINESS FRANCE

A Practical Guide to Understanding French Business Culture

Peggy Kenna   Sondra Lacy

Printed on recyclable paper

PASSPORT BOOKS
a division of *NTC Publishing Group*
Lincolnwood, Illinois USA

Library of Congress Cataloging-in-Publication Data

Kenna, Peggy.
    Business France: a practical guide to understanding French business
culture / Peggy Kenna, Sondra Lacy.
        p.   cm.
    ISBN 0-8442-3554-7
    1. Business etiquette—France.   2. Corporate culture—France.
    3. Business communication—France.   4. Negotiation in business—
    France.   I. Lacy, Sondra.   II. Title.
HF5389.K453   1994
395' .52'0944—dc20   93—40572
                                                        CIP

Published by Passport Books, a division of NTC Publishing Group.
4255 West Touhy Avenue, Lincolnwood, (Chicago) Illinois 60646-1975, U.S.A.
©1994 by NTC Publishing Group. All rights reserved.
No part of this work may be reproduced, stored in a retrieval system
or transmitted in any form or by any means,
electronic or mechanical, including photocopying and recording and otherwise
without the prior permission of NTC Publishing Group.
Manufactured in the United States of America.

4 5 6 7 8 9 0 VP 9 8 7 6 5 4 3 2 1

Contents

Peggy Kenna is a communication specialist working with foreign-born professionals in the American workplace. She provides cross-cultural training and consultation services to companies conducting business internationally. She is also a certified speech and language pathologist who specializes in accent modification. Peggy lives in Tempe, Arizona.

Sondra Lacy is a certified communications specialist and teaches American communication skills to foreign-born professionals in the American workplace. She also provides cross-cultural training and consultation services to companies conducting business internationally. Sondra lives in Scottsdale, Arizona.

Business France is an invaluable tool for thousands of entrepreneurs, businesspeople, corporate executives, technicians, and salespeople seeking to develop lasting business relationships in France.

The book provides a fast, easy way for you to become acquainted with business practices and protocol to help you increase your chances for success in France. You will discover the secrets of doing business internationally while improving your interpersonal communication skills.

Let this book work for you.

> Pam Del Duca
> President/CEO
> The DELSTAR Group
> Scottsdale, Arizona

Entrepreneur Of The Year®
Award Recipient

Welcome to Business France

Business France offers a smooth and problem-free transition between the American and French business cultures.

This pocket-size book contains information you need when traveling in France or doing business with French colleagues. It explains the differences in business culture you will encounter in such areas as:

- Business etiquette

- Communication style

- Problem solving and decision making

- Meetings and presentation style

Business France gets you started on the right track and challenges you to seek ways to improve your success in the global marketplace by understanding cultural differences in the ways people communicate and do business with each other.

Successful international companies are able to adapt to the business styles acceptable in other countries and by other nationalities, based on their knowledge and awareness of key cultural differences. These differences, if not acknowledged and addressed, can adversely affect the success of any business attempting to expand internationally.

Business France is designed to overcome such difficulties by comparing the American culture with the culture of France. Identifying appropriate behavior in one's own culture can make it easier to adapt to that of the country with which you are doing business. With this in mind, the book's unique parallel layout allows an at-a-glance comparison of French business practices with those of the United States.

Practical and easy to use, *Business France* will help you win the confidence of French associates and achieve common business goals.

The global business environment today is a multicultural one. While general business considerations are essentially the same the world over, business styles differ greatly from country to country. What is customary and appropriate in one country may be considered unusual or even offensive in another. The increasingly competitive environment calls for an individual approach to each national market. The success of your venture outside your home market depends largely upon preparation. The American style of business is not universally accepted. Yet we send our employees, executives, salespeople, technicians to negotiate or carry out contracts with little or no understanding of the cultural differences in the ways people communicate and do business with each other. How many business deals have been lost because of this cultural myopia?

Globalization is a process which is drawing people together from all nations of the world into a single community linked by the vast network of communication technologies. Technological breakthroughs in the past two decades have made instant communication between individuals around the world an affordable reality.

As these technological advances continue to open up and expand the dialogue among members of the world community, the need for effective communication between nations and peoples has accelerated.

When change occurs as dramatically and rapidly as we have witnessed in the past decade, many people throughout the world are being forced to quickly learn and adapt to unfamiliar ways of doing things. Some actually welcome change and the opportunities it presents, while others are reluctant to give up familiar ways of doing things. History proves that cultures are slow to change. But, individuals who are mentally prepared to accept change and deal with differences can successfully adapt to cultures very different from their own.

A culture develops when individuals have common experiences and share their reactions to these experiences by communicating with other members of their society.

Over time, communication becomes the vehicle by which cultural beliefs and values are developed, shared and transmitted from one generation to the next. Communication and culture are mutually dependent.

Effective communication between governments or international businesses requires more than being able to speak the language fluently or relying on expert interpreters. Understanding the language is only the first step. Understanding and accepting the behaviors, customs and attitudes of other cultures while interacting globally is also required to bring harmony and success in the worldwide business and political arena.

Doing Business in a Global Market

The importance of the influence of one's native culture on the way one approaches life cannot be overstated. Each country's cultural beliefs and values are reflected in its people's idea of the "right" way to live and behave.

In general, businesspeople who practice low-key, non-adversarial, win/win techniques in doing business abroad tend to be most successful. Knowing what your company wants to achieve, its bottom line, and also understanding the objectives of the other party and helping to accommodate them in the business transaction are necessary for developing long-term, international business relationships.

Often, representatives from American companies, for example, have difficulty doing business with *each other*, even when they speak the same language and share a common culture. Consider how much more difficult it is to do business with people from different cultures who speak different languages.

Success in the international business arena will not be easy for those who do not take steps to gain the skills necessary to be global players. The language barrier is an obvious problem.

Equally important will be negotiation skills, as well as an understanding of and adaptation to the social and business etiquette of the foreign country. Americans have a reputation for failing to appreciate this. In other words, businesspeople doing business abroad will get off to a good start if they remember to do the following:

- Listen closely; understand the verbal and non-verbal communications.
- Focus on mutual interests, not differences.
- Nurture long-term relationships.
- Emphasize quality. Be prepared to defend the quality of your products and services, and the quality of your business relationship.

ISO 9000 is fast becoming a universal passport for doing business in Europe. ISO stands for International Organization for Standardization.

This is a new set of concise standards covering documented quality control systems for product development, design, production, management and inspection.

The European Economic Community (EEC) has adopted ISO certification and more than 20,000 European companies are complying. Increasing numbers of European companies are refusing to do business with foreign suppliers who don't meet ISO standards. Product areas under the most pressure to comply include automotive, aerospace, electronics, testing and measuring instruments, and products where safety and reliability can become an issue. Companies with Total Quality Management (TQM) in place find it easier to pass ISO 9000 audits.

Successful companies will need to adapt to these rules and standards set by Europe in order to do business there.

Total Quality Management is becoming an integral part of successful companies in the United States.

TQM is an organized, company-wide effort to eliminate waste in every aspect of business and to produce the highest quality product possible. TQM is a philosophy that focuses on the customer, manages by facts, empowers people and improves processes.

Implementation of this process is a real challenge and requires a company commitment to invest the time and finances necessary to reshape the entire organization. How is this accomplished? Through a team approach which values customer and employee opinions and in which everyone is committed to identify waste and its root cause and correct it in a timely manner. An effective tool for accomplishing this is through brainstorming efforts allowing everyone to participate. The successful TQM company is customer driven and uses leadership, information and analysis, strategic quality planning, human resource utilization, and quality assurance of products and services to reach goals.

Total Quality Management is a survival tool for businesses in a global market.

One of the largest countries in Western Europe, France is fiercely proud of its history as a political and cultural leader. The French people remain determined to preserve their artistic and historical heritage, maintain a place as a world economic power, and retain a high standard of living.

A close relationship has long existed between the French government and its larger industries, with cooperation and subsidization a common arrangement. Industry finds many of its leaders among the graduates of the schools which supply the elite corps of civil servants.

Education is entirely state controlled and supported and is a top priority in France. Social status and career are influenced by the school one attended and how well one did.

Although foreign investment is closely controlled and monitored by the government, there is still much foreign investment in French industry. French labor laws are extensive and comprehensive and are designed to protect the employee.

France is a leading proponent of economic planning. Corporate strategic planning is far-reaching and detailed. The larger the company the more elaborate the planning and the longer the time frame.

French women are joining the workforce increasingly. Many are joining businesses, especially in service industries, and work in staff positions. They are fighting for equality, and many French men still feel somewhat uncomfortable with women executives.

Remember that within every culture, there are still individual differences among people and organizations. Be prepared to find specific exceptions to the general trends within a culture.

Communication Style

United States

■ *Fact oriented*

Americans tend to be factual and inductive. They worry about presenting their data clearly and are less concerned with the thought process.

They like summaries and often give the conclusion first and then tell how that conclusion was reached.

Americans tend to be pragmatic. They value ideas which are practical and useful with a stress on consequences. They see events as occurring in a linear chain of cause and effect.

Americans write detailed letters with all facts and plans and like to give a sense of completion.

■ *Cartesian logic*

Cartesian logic stresses abstract thinking and the use of statistics and figures. It is not fact oriented but instead looks for patterns. The French like to do an in-depth analysis and argue every point; they break a subject into its component parts, analyze each part and then put it all back together again. It often seems they are talking in circles before they come to a decision. They don't like prepared summaries. Well presented logic is the key to reach the French. The most persuasive argument to the French is the logical, practical argument.

The French like to have new proposals built up slowly, allowing time for them to digest information and ideas. They also want to know the background of the presenter to establish credibility.

French written communication often tends to be tentative and cumulative. Letters are often full of subtleties, with each letter elaborating upon the previous letter. They also tend to write long letters with elaborate introductory and closing paragraphs and are formal in tone.

United States

■ *Informal style*

Americans tend to be very informal and start calling each other by first names almost immediately. They also tend to dress more informally.

Informality and a casual appearance are seen as signs of warmth and equality.

■ *Fewer interruptions*

Americans tend to do only one thing at a time – they either talk or listen. This is particularly true in business.

■ *Moderately expressive*

Americans like direct eye contact but dislike "staring." They use some hand gestures; how many depends on the individual.

■ *More formal*

To the French, style (both in dress and manners) is very important. It is the overall effect that matters to the French, not the details. They are much more formal than Americans both in dress and in the use of first names. They do not get on a first name basis quickly.

Informality can be seen as intrusive and can result in loss of respect.

■ *Constant interruptions*

The French like to do many things at the same time and will constantly interrupt each other. It will often seem like everyone talks at the same time and no one listens. This occurs in business as well as social settings.

■ *Very expressive*

The French use more intense eye contact than Americans are used to. They also tend to use a lot of hand gestures.

Communication Style

United States

■ *Prefer action*

Americans usually prefer action (doing something) to exchanging opinions. Americans also don't tend to appreciate historical and scholarly references. Americans like to state their purpose right away and want to get immediately to business. They like both written and oral presentations to be brief and easily understandable.

When they do converse Americans often use superlatives and conversation frequently contains the word "I." Some do a lot of boasting and have a tendency to exaggerate.

Americans use small talk in both business and social settings. It is used to acknowledge the other person and develop rapport. Some, but not all Americans, find debate on issues stimulating but most want to resolve differences as quickly as possible to get on with business.

■ *Like discussion*

The French pride themselves on the art of speaking their language with great precision, fluency and wit. Repartee (witty or clever retorts) is greatly admired. They like to use scholarly references when speaking. This is also true in writing. The ability to use language well is considered the mark of an intelligent, educated person. Bragging or boasting is considered immature and a sign of weakness.

The French like small talk but tend to leave some things to the imagination. They admire sophistication, learning and nuance. The French relish conflict and spirited discussions but rhetoric must be logical and well presented. They can be friendly, humorous and sarcastic and often criticize institutions, conditions and the people they live with. An exchange of differing views is considered stimulating.

United States

■ *Directive management*

In American companies, someone is always in charge and there is a clear decision maker. Someone is always held accountable and expectations are clear. Decisions do tend to go from the top down but decision makers are found at all levels depending on the importance of the decision. Managers at lower levels often get a chance to provide input. Americans believe those closest to a problem should have input in determining the solution.

Americans are procedures oriented. Employees like to have job descriptions and know specifically what they are responsible for.

■ *Authoritarian management*

Managers exert strong control over subordinates and expect obedience from everyone. Subordinates, however, feel free to criticize and argue with leaders. French executives can and do make independent decisions. They sometimes don't keep their subordinates well informed and may not delegate much.

Decision making is highly centralized and made after much deliberation. The French believe that taking time to make decisions is prudent.

There tends to be many layers of middle management and French companies can be slow to respond to change and varying conditions. They are very cautious.

French managers often share information only with people of equal status and not with employees. They also tend not to delegate. Supervisors can be good at pointing out mistakes and uneasy with giving compliments.

The French are not as procedures oriented as Americans.

United States

■ *Status*

Power is more important than status and power is not always indicated by title, maturity or education; it can be determined by force of personality.

Americans are impressed by a person's achievements. Material wealth is also a sign of success.

Americans want to be liked and are very sensitive to praise or blame. They tend to like people who agree with them.

■ *Promotions*

In the upper ranks of management, promotion is often not based on technical expertise or competence but instead is based on things like good management skills, ability to "play the game," and political knowledge.

■ *Relationships short term*

To Americans business relationships are not personal. They do not spend much time building a relationship. Also, constant changes within companies make it unlikely that one person will remain in a position long enough to build long-term relationships. Relationships in a business transaction can be very confrontational at times but this is not expected to have an adverse affect. Americans are inclined to trust easily.

■ *Status*

Background degrees, awards, and the schools you attend are very important.

Business cards are more likely to contain degrees earned than job titles which are felt to be temporary anyway.

The French tend to gain recognition and create their identity by thinking and acting in opposition to (arguing with) others.

■ *Promotions*

Respect for authority is based on respect for competence, especially technical competence. Education is the primary gateway to success in French companies.

■ *Relationships important*

The French like to establish personal business relationships. Personal contacts are crucial for doing business in France. It is especially important to establish personal relationships at the highest levels of the hierarchy. The French usually build trust slowly; it must be earned.

Karen

United States

■ *Constant change*

Americans believe in constant change. This often causes hierarchies and relationships to be repeatedly disrupted. The needs of the individual are considered subsidiary to the organization. Loyalty between employee and company is temporary but expected to be wholehearted while it lasts.

Americans attach much importance to achievement. Therefore decision making occurs at levels where results allow managers to reach quantifiable goals.

■ *Planning*

Americans spend much time and effort planning concepts and establishing procedures to carry out the plan. Success or failure depends on the agreed-upon plan. Planning is usually from the top down but can be bottom up. Planning in American companies requires interpersonal skills. Planning tends to be short term.

Work and what one does for a living is a primary part of how Americans define themselves. Most Americans have difficulty balancing work with lifestyle and personal goals. Often work will take precedence.

■ *Centralized and hierarchical*

There is not nearly as much change in French companies as in American companies. French society is divided into clearly defined classes: aristocracy and high level managers; middle level people such as teachers, middle managers, shopkeepers and artisans; and workers and low level employees. Everything in France is centralized. And French organizations reflect this; top management doesn't always keep lower levels of management informed about decisions.

■ *Planning*

Planning is done centrally and tends to be inductive (specific to general). Because managers may not be included in the planning, this can result in their not taking ownership of the plan and not being committed to implementing it since they had no input.

The French like to engage in long-term planning but it is very difficult for them since they are very well aware of all the things that can happen to interfere with the plan. They also believe that life is to enjoy now and do not spend all their time working.

Organizational Structure

United States

■ *Risk takers*

Americans tend to make decisions quickly and easily. While accuracy is important, they believe a person can learn from failure and should take risks. It is OK to take chances and learn from mistakes. They also believe criticism should be objective but tactful. Risk taking and competition are primary methods of motivation.

■ *More open*

Detailed written contracts are standard although an oral agreement carries weight as a preliminary agreement. Americans can be creative about financial statements; they are required by law to publish a financial statement.

■ *Problem solving*

Americans often use a brainstorming technique. They feel that there is usually more than one solution to a problem and want to choose the most efficient. American logic tends to be deductive (go from generalizations to specifics).

France

■ *Not risk takers*

The French tend to be cautious and take their time reaching a decision. The French are highly competitive with each other but are also very sensitive to being wrong. Mistakes are not well tolerated and also cause a person to "lose face."

■ *Secretive*

Only written commitments are binding to the French. To be sure of something, get it in writing. It is best not to take at face value financial statements or assurances about a French business. They are very secretive about financial matters. They also feel Americans are too concerned with money and lack creativity as a result.

communic
Karen

■ *Problem solving*

The French like formal studies and reports. They then circulate these reports for individual study and comment. They don't really like oral presentations or discussions to disseminate information. They like reports to be comprehensive, clear, well structured, well written and well presented. They tend to be inductive (go from particulars to generalizations) and very positive.

United States

■ *Impatient*

Americans tend to be very impatient. They want to get down to business right away. They establish relationships quickly and the relationship is usually only temporary until business is completed.

■ *Very schedule oriented*

Americans like fixed agendas and schedules when meeting. They feel it is important to keep appointments. Work schedules are planned and usually adhered to.

■ *Patient*

The French are more patient than Americans. They view time as an ally in negotiations. They like everything to proceed at a moderate pace. Meetings often last late into the evening.

■ *Dislike strict schedules*

The French don't always adhere to schedules or appointments. They think nothing of changing plans at the last minute. The French also feel that taking time to make decisions is a sign of prudence. Americans sometimes complain about French delays in deliveries, their failure to submit routine reports on schedule and their easy tendency to interrupt work schedules.

Punctuality

United States

■ *Punctuality considered polite*

It is very important to be on time for all appointments. This includes social activities.

Americans see time as divided into segments to be completed. There is a beginning time and ending time for each section of a day.

■ *Fast pace*

Americans like incessant activity. They start the day early and usually have short lunches. They like "doing." Americans tend to make quick decisions about business and believe in quick planning and implementation. They feel that any problems or mistakes can be fixed as they arise. Quick decision makers are valued provided they are usually right.

■ *Use time as a weapon*

Punctuality in business and social invitations is important. However, the French may keep you waiting to gain a negotiating edge or to indicate that they don't like your proposals. They may set an appointment and then still keep that person waiting for over an hour. This is to show their authority and it also makes them look busy. However, it is best to be punctual when attending a meeting with the French.

■ *Slower pace*

The French start work later in the morning but often work late into the evening. They take long lunch breaks which start later than in the U.S. Etiquette also dictates that one should be a little late (5-10 minutes) if invited out for dinner. This shows that the guest is not overly anxious.

United States

■ *Action oriented*

Americans tend to stick to the issue and become impatient with digressions. While Americans like to debate, especially in informal meetings, they are primarily concerned with the results of the meeting and like to have action items assigned to participants. Everyone is encouraged to present opinions and then the majority rules.

■ *Businesslike and impersonal*

Americans like to get right down to business since meetings are usually tightly scheduled and have fixed agendas. They are not particularly interested in established, long-term relationships. They will establish rapport with a minimum of small talk.

Americans feel that questioning does not imply criticism and says nothing about the competence of the person. It can simply indicate high interest or it can indicate that an individual act is being questioned, not the whole character of the person.

■ *Love to argue*

The French will often sacrifice contents for form. The result of a meeting may not be as important as the way it was arrived at. Even when they basically agree with your point of view, the French still like to argue, expand on all aspects of the subject, and interrupt at any time during the conversation. The French highly admire individualism and feel it is important that each participant have the opportunity to present a point of view. Even when they all agree with each other, they like to see how each individual presents arguments.

■ *Personal relationships valued*

The French do not usually get right down to business. They like to visit first and get a feeling for the general mood.

The French are a very proud and sensitive people. A foreigner must be very tactful and courteous. To question a proposal or idea is to question the competence of the person who put it forward. Brainstorming meetings are not common. This is done informally before the meeting.

United States

■ *Criticism constructive*

Americans believe criticism can be constructive and that this type of criticism should not affect relationships. They believe there is a difference between criticism of a person and criticism of that person's work.

■ *Like agendas*

Some meetings are brainstorming sessions; some are to disseminate information; some are to discuss, defend and decide.

Americans like fixed agendas and schedules. Americans want to get down to business right away. Meetings can become very heated with many confrontations and disagreements to be resolved. Because of time constraints a meeting may be adjourned before all business is completed. Americans always want to leave a meeting with some kind of action plan.

■ *Dislike criticism*

The French dislike being criticized and don't like having mistakes pointed out or being rigorously questioned. Face saving is important.

■ *Dislike agendas*

The goal in a meeting is to assess and brief participants, inform and be informed, feel out people's reactions and encourage expression of opinions. The tempo will be fast with prolonged discussions of many things. Participants are eloquent and much of the discussion may seem to be irrelevant. There will be many interruptions and digressions. A detailed agenda is usually provided at a meeting but it is seldom followed. Usually there will be no action plan as the decision maker is not at the meeting. When scheduling a series of meetings for the French, allow twice as much time as you would for Americans.

United States

■ *Presentations*

Americans tend to like a projecting style of speaking. They will often combine informative and persuasive styles as an efficient method of presentation. They attempt to persuade the audience to make a decision or take an action at the same time as they provide information. They consider this an effective and efficient use of time. They expect the audience to ask questions and test the presenter's knowledge. Presenters are expected to defend their opinions.

Americans also like to have frequent summaries and often tend to present their conclusions first and then follow up with how conclusions were reached.

■ *Presentations*

French presentations are often elaborate, long-winded and emotional, and filled with literary and historical allusions. They like to enhance their main theme with elaborate tangents. They will often provide masses of figures organized in complex patterns along with detailed background information. The French like to debate and will interrupt during a presentation with arguments that may or may not seem relevant to the topic being discussed. To deal with constant interruptions a presentation should be organized so it can be delivered in small segments.

The French like reason and logic and will look at presentations to see if they are logical, factual, rational and well argued. Conclusions are less important. Presentations tend to be formal, informative, rational and subdued.

United States

■ *Value independence*

While Americans value their independence, they also work fairly well in teams. Teams are both competitive and cooperative. Americans feel self esteem can be increased by cooperating with others. Teams are formed for a short period of time to accomplish a specific goal and then disbanded. Since Americans do not commit wholeheartedly to a group, individuals can work on a number of teams.

Americans tend to see individualism as self reliance.

■ *Value individuality*

Teams are seen as a collaboration of specialists chosen for their competence and under the command of an unequivocal leader. There is often more rivalry than collaboration. The French don't tend to be strong on teamwork. They can be very competitive and do not tend to wait for group consensus to take the initiative. They also like strong leadership but will often challenge and contradict this leader. French labor laws are very employee oriented and give workers much more protection.

United States

■ *Competitive*

Americans are competitive and want to get the best deal They can be fairly flexible in order to conclude a business transaction. They also tend to be more spontaneous in their approach to negotiations and are often fairly informal. They believe in compromise and that there are universal rules of competition or fair play.

Americans believe that debate over issues is very acceptable but they do not believe in arguing just for the sake of discussion.

■ *Risk takers*

Americans believe that change and progress are good. They like new ideas.

■ *Value "fair play"*

Americans believe that there are rules of fair play and that all everyone should be treated the same. They believe both parties to a contract should be held equally responsible for abiding by its terms.

■ *Argumentative*

The French love of the abstract doesn't lend itself to negotiation, bargaining and compromise. They tend to dislike the type of face-to-face discussion such as negotiations which lead to compromise. They also dislike the hard sell. They often have an elaborate, well prepared opening position but few fallback positions.

The French like to disagree for the sake of discussion. They normally state their intention openly and directly and get to the point quickly.

■ *Dislike change*

The French are not risk takers. They are essentially conservative. If presenting new ideas to them, make sure you have done your research well.

■ *Value loyalty to France*

French law is designed to protect French business. Don't expect it to provide impartial treatment for foreign companies. The French tend to abide by a contract only as long as it suits them but hold foreigners rigidly to it. Taking time to build a relationship of trust with a French company will usually lead them to provide more impartial and fair treatment.

Negotiating

United States

■ *Fast paced*

Americans do not usually anticipate long term negotiations. They like fast-paced negotiations and also tend to attack issues sequentially, resolving one issue at a time. They are very interested in the technical aspects of negotiation. Decisions are often made quickly. Not all decisions need to be made by executives; sometimes lower level managers can make decisions. Sometimes their impatience can lead Americans to make unnecessary concessions.

Punctuality is important. Americans will seldom be more than a few minutes late to a meeting or negotiation session. They also expect others to be equally punctual.

■ *Informal*

Americans are more informal than the French. They like to quickly get to first-name basis and an informal atmosphere. They often use humor if they feel negotiations are stalled in an attempt to lighten the atmosphere..

■ *Slower paced*

The French will take more time when negotiating. They are very analytical and decisions are made only after much deliberation. Decisions also must go up the hierarchy.

Don't be surprised (or upset) if the French aren't particularly punctual. They, on the other hand, expect the other party to be on time. Being late can hurt negotiations with the French.

■ *Formal and distant*

The French tend to be more formal and distant than Americans. Dressing well and using good manners is very important. They like people who have a sense of style. They like to be addressed formally, not by first names, and joking during negotiations is not common.

U.S. Business Etiquette

- Be punctual. Americans are very time conscious. They also tend to conduct business at a fairly fast pace.

- A firm handshake and direct eye contact is the standard greeting.

- Direct eye contact is very important in business. Not making eye contact implies boredom or disinterest.

- Gift giving is not common. The United States has bribery laws which restrict the value of gifts which can be given.

- The United States is not particularly rank and status conscious. Titles are not used when addressing executives. Americans usually like to use first names very quickly. Informality tends to be equated with equality.

- Business meetings usually start with a formal agenda and tasks to be accomplished. There is usually very little small talk. Participants are expected to express their ideas openly; disagreements are common.

- Permission should be asked before smoking.

- If there is no one to introduce you in a business meeting, you may introduce yourself and present your card.

French Business Etiquette

- The French are formal and conservative in business protocol. The French usually dress very conservatively. This is changing somewhat but it is best to be conservative until you discover if your counterparts are dressing more informally.

- First names are rarely used. Also if you do speak any French, always use the formal "you" (vous) and not the informal (tu).

- Plan to exchange business cards frequently.

- Avoid personal questions, politics, money and religion.

- The French dislike using the word "I" and tend to shun boasting.

- The French dislike a lot of touching.

- Privacy is very important to the French and they tend to separate business and social life.

- Introductions are formal. Handshakes are light and quick. You are also expected to greet everyone in the room. Shake hands every time you meet a person. Do not use first names until they ask you to.

Remember that the word etiquette comes from the French.

- Americans tend to stand an arms length away from each other.

- Americans generally respect queues or lines. To shove or push one's way into a line will often result in anger and verbal complaint.

- Beckoning is done by raising the index finger and curling it in and out, or by raising the hand and curling the fingers back toward the body.

- Using the hand and index finger to point at objects or to point directions is common.

- Whistling is a common way to get the attention of someone at a distance.

- "No" is signalled by waving the forearm and hand (palm out) in front and across the upper body, back and forth.

- Americans use the standard OK sign, the V for victory sign and the thumbs up sign.

- The OK sign means zero.

- The French do not use lines or queues in the same way Americans do. Some pushing and shoving to get to the front is acceptable.

- It is not polite to point with the hand and fingers.

- When the French shrug with the shoulders, palms extended, it means "It doesn't worry me." If the palms are chest high, it means "What do you expect me to do about it?"

- Pointing to the eye means "You can't fool me."

- Flicking the fingers across the cheek, means "How dull."

- Avoid the following gestures:
    - resting feet on tables or chairs
    - using toothpicks, nail clippers, combs in public,
    - conversing with hands in pockets
    - yawning or scratching in public
    - loud conversations in public
    - snapping fingers of both hands simultaneously
    - slapping open palm over closed fist (vulgar)

Communication Interferences

Effective communication, both verbal and nonverbal, means that the sending and processing of information between people, countries and businesses is understood, examined, interpreted, and responded to in some way. Any factor that causes a barrier or eliminates the successful transmission of information is defined as a communication interference.

- **Environmental interference** is an actual physical disturbance in the environment such as power outage, unregulated temperatures, a person or group talking very loud, etc.

- **Physiological interference** can be a hearing loss, laryngitis, illness, stuttering, neurological or organic deficit, etc.

- **Semantic interference.** We understand a word to have a certain meaning but the other person has a different meaning. Body language and gestures mean different things to different people. This includes confusion of abbreviated organizational jargon and pronunciation. Universal meanings (semantic understanding) are rare.

- **Syntactic interference.** Words are placed in certain order to give our language meaning. If the words are out of order, the meaning may be changed (this includes grammar).

- **Organizational interference.** Ideas being discussed lack sequence and can't be followed.

- **Psychological interference.** Words that incite emotion are used. In any emotional state (positive or negative) emotions need to be diffused in order to communicate effectively.

- **Social interference.** This includes cultural manners that are inappropriate for the country such as accepted codes for dress, business etiquette, communication rules, social activity.

Always become well informed about the customs and culture and get information before you try and do business in another country. Review this book and decide which areas of communication you and your colleagues will have difficulty with in France. Anticipate and plan accordingly.

As the visitor to another country, you need to move out of your "comfort zone." Make the people from another country feel comfortable doing business with you.

No one country has a lock on world markets. Fundamental changes have occurred in the world economy in the last decade. New technologies and low labor costs often give nations that once were not major players an advantage. This results in increased competition. Yet international business is vital to any country's prosperity.

Business is conducted by people and the future of any country in a global economy will lie with people who can effectively think and act across ethnic, cultural and language barriers. We need to understand that the differences between nations and cultures is profound. The European-based culture of the United States has very different values and behaviors than other cultures in the world. If you cannot accept and adapt to these differences, you will not succeed.

Companies striving to market their business overseas can become truly successful only when they recognize that the key is operating with sensitivity toward the culture and communication of the other country. Communication cannot be separated from culture and this is true when doing business in other countries.

No flourishing company would present themselves to another company in the same country without researching that company's business culture and then adapting their image to meet the customer's comfort level. It's the same when doing business in another country. You must adapt your image by using your knowledge of effective cultural communication to present a positive public image to the other country.

The first thing is to identify your target audience: clients, customers, suppliers, financial people, government employees and so on. Then you must learn how to effectively communicate with them, and this means learning the culture.

Business failure internationally rarely results from technical or professional incompetence. It is often due to a lack of understanding of what people from other countries want, how they work and so on. This lack of understanding can put a company at a tremendous disadvantage.

Learning the business protocol and practices of the country where you want to do business can give you great leverage. The more you know about the people you do business with, the more successful you can be. Businesspeople need to make every contact they have with a foreign customer or business partner a positive one. Business leaders and managers must rethink the way they do business in the new global marketplace.

To be successful in the global market, you must:

- **Be flexible.** Adapting to differences in culture is necessary for individuals from both countries to get along and do business. Resisting the local culture will only lead to distrust.

- **Have patience.** Adjust your planning. Initiating business in many countries takes a long-range approach and may require two or three years. Anticipate problems and develop alternative strategies.

- **Prepare thoroughly.** Research the country, the organization, the culture and beliefs of the people you will be dealing with.

- **Know your bottom line.** Know exactly what you want from a deal and at what point an agreement is not in your best interest. Know when to walk away.

- **Show respect.** Search for the other side's needs and interests. Accentuate the positive. Don't preach your own beliefs, and respect their beliefs.

- **Form relationships.** Encourage getting involved with the new community if you are going to be in the country for a long period.

■ **Keep your cool.** Pay attention to the wide range of national, cultural, religious and social differences you encounter.

When you are using this book, review your own beliefs and values about correct business protocol and ethics. Then match these ideas with the business practices and protocol in France.

You can contribute to your own success by recognizing that you will have to move out of your own "comfort zone" of doing business into the cultural business zone of France in order to develop the rapport necessary to meet the needs of your client or partner. This does not mean you compromise your company's image or product but that you do business following France's protocol while there. It's only for a short time that you may be following their rules, and the payoff can be one in which concepts can be sold while still maintaining a consistent image and approach that is culturally appropriate.

Quick Tips: United States

- The United States is a very ethnically diverse country. To do business, it is important to be open to this diversity and to be flexible.

- Americans tend to be very individually oriented and concerned with their own careers. Their first loyalty is to themselves.

- Americans want to be liked. The prefer people who are good team players and want to cooperate.

- Americans value equality and dislike people who are too status or rank conscious.

- Most Americans are open, friendly, casual and informal in their manners. They like to call people by their first name quickly.

- Americans like to come right to the point and are uncomfortable with people who are indirect and subtle. They like a direct and specific "yes" or "no."

- Americans expect people to speak up and give their opinions freely and to be honest in the information they give.

- Americans can be very persistent. When they conclude a business transaction and sign a contract, they expect it to be honored. They do not like people who change their minds later.

- Plan to spend time building long-term relationships. The French are very concerned with relationships in business.

- To sell a product line in France, you must first sell yourself and your company.

- Allow more time for everything in France. Have patience.

- Give your advertising a French flavor.

- The French are very past oriented and proud of their history. The French tend to be chauvinistic about their country and language.

- The French are more Latin in their behavior than they are like Northern Europeans.

- Form is preeminent. Perfection in style and manners is important to the French. Americans must take great care not to alienate the French by being casual and informal in their manners. The French tend to feel Americans don't present themselves very well and are not well rounded. Americans feel French are preoccupied with status, rank and formality.

Common Phrases

Good morning	Bonjour
Good evening	Bonsoir
My name is	Je m'appelle
What's your name?	Comment vouz appelez-vous?
Pleased to meet you	Enchanté
How are you?	Comment allez-vous?
Fine, thank you	Bien, merci
And you?	Et vous?
You are welcome	Je vous en prie
Excuse me	Pardon
Please	S'il vous plait
Yes/No	Oui/Non
Goodbye	Au revoir
Mr/Mrs/Miss	Monsieur/Madame/ Mademoiselle

Notes

Available in this series:

Business China

Business France

Business Germany

Business Japan

Business Mexico

Business Taiwan

For more information, please contact:

Sales and Marketing Department
NTC Publishing Group
4255 West Touhy Avenue
Lincolnwood, IL 60646
708-679-5500